HUMANS IN SPACE

FLIGHT INTO ORBIT

DAVID JEFFERIS AND MAT IRVINE

Crabtree Publishing Company
www.crabtreebooks.com

Introduction

Today, people live and work in space stations, which are spacecraft that circle the Earth more than a dozen times a day. Back when space flight was just a dream, scientists thought that space stations might look like huge wheels. These rotating cities in space would have dozens, perhaps even hundreds of people aboard them.

The reality is very different. The International Space Station (ISS) is certainly big, but it looks like a collection of tin cans bolted together, and is home to no more than a few astronauts at a time. The ISS provides valuable lessons in international teamwork, and experience for future human space exploration.

Crabtree Publishing Company
PMB 16A,
350 Fifth Avenue, suite 3308,
New York, NY 10118

616 Welland Avenue,
St. Catharines,
Ontario L2M 5V6

Coordinating Editor: Ellen Rodger
Project Editors:
Carrie Gleason, Adrianna Morganelli,
L. Michelle Nielsen
Production Coordinator: Rose Gowsell
Prepress technician: Nancy Johnson

© 2007 Crabtree Publishing Company

Educational advisor: Julie Stapleton
Written and produced by:
David Jefferis and Mat Irvine/Buzz Books

©2007 David Jefferis/Buzz Books

Library of Congress
Cataloging-in-Publication Data

Jefferis, David.
  Flight into orbit / written by David Jefferis & Mat Irvine.
    p. cm. -- (Humans in space)
  Includes index.
  ISBN-13: 978-0-7787-3101-6 (rlb)
  ISBN-10: 0-7787-3101-4 (rlb)
  ISBN-13: 978-0-7787-3115-3 (pb)
  ISBN-10: 0-7787-3115-4 (pb)
  1. Astronautics--History--Juvenile literature. 2. Manned space
flight--History--Juvenile literature. I. Irvine, Mat. II. Title. III. Series.

TL793.J4196 2007
629.45'4--dc22

2007003600

Pictures from below, clockwise:
1 An astronaut working in space.
2 A 1950s space station concept.
3 Station assembly work, high above Earth.
4 Anousheh Ansari, the first female **space tourist**.
5 A U.S. Space Shuttle roars off the launch pad.

Contents

Circling the Earth

The idea of a "city in the sky" dates back more than a hundred years. Today, the huge International Space Station (ISS) is a permanently crewed structure in orbit.

▲ Edward Everett Hale wrote *The Brick Moon* in 1869. It is thought to be the first book to talk about humans living in orbit.

The International Space Station follows a curving path around the Earth, called an orbit. The ISS travels continuously in this near-circular course, completing a single orbit once every 90 to 93 minutes.

In orbit, the ISS travels at 17,200 miles per hour (27,700 kilometers per hour). That is a speed of almost five miles (eight kilometers) *each second*. The speed is an balancing act – any faster and the ISS will fly further away, any slower and it will fall to Earth.

▶ The International Space Station has been occupied continuously since the first crew went aboard in 2000.

The first spacecraft in orbit

The world's first **artificial satellite** was **Sputnik 1**, which was fired into space in 1957.

Sputnik 1 was a 23-inch (58-centimeter) metal sphere, weighing 184 pounds (83.6 kilograms). Four long **antennas** on the satellite transmitted radio signals to the world. The "beep-beep" noises heard on Earth and made by this first spacecraft made Sputnik 1 the top news story across the world.

Sputnik 1 stayed in space for just over three months. During that time it completed 1440 orbits around the Earth.

A postage stamp showed Sputnik 1 and a future space station

Sputnik's radio antenna

The orbital height of the ISS varies between about 200 to 218 miles (320 to 350 kilometers)

◄ The ISS follows an **inclined orbit** as it circles the Earth. This means that the ISS orbits somewhere between the **equator** and the poles. The Earth also turns on its axis, once every 24 hours, so ISS crews see a constantly changing panorama of the world as they speed overhead.

The ISS orbit is inclined at 51.6 degrees to the equator

► There are many orbital paths around the Earth. Ones high above the equator are used to relay TV and radio signals.

Orbital height is how high up a satellite is. The ISS orbits Earth at a height of about 218 miles (350 kilometers). From time to time it needs a rocket boost to maintain this orbit, otherwise it would eventually graze the upper **atmosphere** and crash.

Various spacecraft, including the U.S. **Space Shuttle** and the Russian **Soyuz**, fly to and from the ISS, carrying construction materials, new crews, and supplies.

► The U.S. Space Shuttle *Atlantis* is shown here linked to Mir, a Russian space station that orbited the Earth from 1986 to 2001.

The first space stations

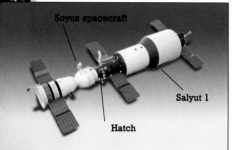

Soyuz spacecraft

Salyut 1

Hatch

▲ Salyut 1 was fitted with **life-support** systems for a three-man crew. Cosmonauts entered through the hatch.

Long before the International Space Station, Russia launched Salyut, or "Salute," 1 into orbit. This truck-sized metal cylinder was the world's first space station.

Salyut 1 was fired into space on April 19, 1971. Four days later, **cosmonauts** in a Soyuz spacecraft tried to board the empty station. The entry hatch did not work properly, and they could not get inside. Later attempts were successful, and Salyut 1 was occupied for 24 of the 175 days it spent in orbit. As a test for bigger stations to come, Salyut 1 was a great success.

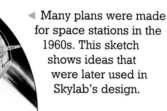

◄ Many plans were made for space stations in the 1960s. This sketch shows ideas that were later used in Skylab's design.

The U.S. Skylab was another early space station. It was an empty fuel tank fitted with an entry hatch and equipment for three astronauts to live in space. When Skylab launched in May 1973, various pieces of equipment were damaged. Astronauts made repairs, and three crews spent more than 170 days total on board.

▼ Skylab's designers solved many problems of living in space. This compact dining table allowed three astronauts to eat and drink together.

Astronomy instruments
were carried in
this section

ORBITFACT
Salyut 1 was the first of seven similar-looking space stations launched by Russia over twenty years, until 1991. Mir was next, and was the longest-lasting space station. It was discarded because Russia decided to join the ISS project.

Mir, or "Peace," was Russia's largest space station. It was assembled over a ten-year period, between 1986 and 1996. Mir normally housed three crew members, but up to six sometimes stayed. In 2001 the station was abandoned, and allowed to re-enter the atmosphere. It broke up, or fell apart, over the Pacific Ocean.

Super-size space wheel

2001: A Space Odyssey was a realistic-looking science fiction movie. This 1968 film showed an impressive space station, used in the movie as a stop-off point for flights to the Moon.

The space station in the movie was far beyond anything we could build today. The fictional wheel-shaped station was huge.

One of the biggest differences between the movie and reality is the look of the interiors. In *2001: A Space Odyssey*, the space station is roomy. It even has an elegant hotel on board. In reality, space stations are packed full of equipment, looking more like the inside of an old-fashioned submarine.

The entry hatch
for spacecraft

A futuristic space shuttle design

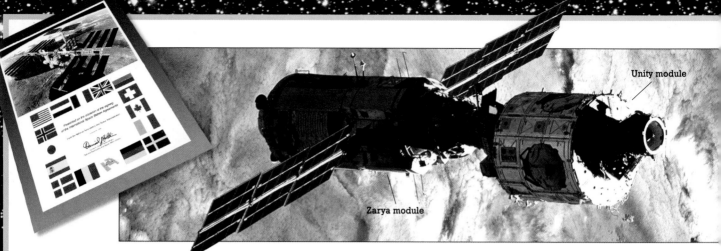

Unity module

Zarya module

Island in the sky

△ The ISS project is run by the **space agencies** of Canada, Europe, Japan, Russia, and the U.S. Other countries are also involved, and work through these agencies.

The International Space Station (ISS) is a project that uses the skills of many nations. It is the largest human-made object in space.

The ISS is built of various units, called **modules**, which are assembled in space, piece by piece. The first modules were launched into orbit in 1998, when the ISS was little bigger than a large truck. Now it is huge, and still growing. It is home to crews of three, for stays of six months at a time. The number of people can vary. During an assembly mission a docked Shuttle and the ISS share a crew of up to ten people.

△ In 1998 the ISS consisted of just the Russian-built Zarya and the U.S. Unity modules.

▶ By 2006, the ISS looked like this. The **main truss** is the backbone of the station. Crewed modules are below the truss.

△ The first ISS crew went aboard in 2000. Here they balance **weightless** oranges for a television transmission to viewers down on Earth.

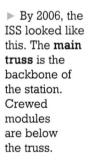

The Phantom Torso

The phantom of the ISS, nicknamed Fred, was no ghost, but a piece of hardware made to react to the space environment like a human body does.

The dangers of space include **radiation**, or invisible particles pouring from the Sun, which can damage or kill living cells. Fred had artificial skin and internal organs, such as a heart, brain, and stomach.

The organs were made of material that would be affected like human organs.

Tests during Fred's stay in 2001 showed that ISS crews were in danger when there is a massive storm or **flare** on the Sun's surface. During this event, astronauts working in space suits outside the ISS must come inside.

When fully built, the ISS will be 361 feet (110 meter) long, roughly the size of a soccer field. The various parts will add up to about 470 tons (426 tonnes), more than three times that of the earlier Mir.

The pictures on these pages show the progress made between 1998 and 2006. Extra modules made the ISS much bigger, but construction delays ensured that there was still much work to be done.

ORBITFACT
The ISS makes its power with huge **solar panels**. These are made of silicon, a material that changes the energy in sunlight to electricity. They also charge batteries, so that when the ISS is in the Earth's shadow, electrical systems continue to work.

Solar panels

Main truss

Crewed module

Heavy lifter

The key to building the ISS is the U.S. Space Shuttle, which carries all the biggest parts from Earth to orbit in its cargo bay.

Space Shuttles are the largest spacecraft to visit the ISS, and are used to take up materials for construction, new crews, and supplies. The crewed part of the Shuttle system is the winged Orbiter **space plane**. At takeoff, the Orbiter is attached to two **solid-rocket boosters** (SRBs) and a big external fuel tank (ET). These are all left behind when their fuel is used up. Only the Orbiter reaches as far as the ISS.

An Orbiter has room for up to seven astronauts, but its massive cargo bay is why it is important for the ISS. The station was designed with the Orbiter in mind as a "space truck." Most modules can be carried in one piece in an Orbiter's long cargo bay.

▲ The Space Shuttle being taken to its launch pad by the world's biggest vehicle, the crawler-transporter.

▲ A complete seven member Space Shuttle crew.

◄ Takeoff uses the combined **thrust** of two solid rocket boosters and three main engines. These use fuel from the huge external tank (arrowed).

▲ The solid boosters parachute into the sea when their fuel is finished. They are recovered, cleaned, and refilled for later use.

The cargo bay doors of a Shuttle Orbiter stay open in space, as they have **radiators** to help keep the Orbiter cool in the Sun's glare. In the bay is an Italian-made Multi-Purpose Logistics Module (MPLM). Three MPLMs have been built, each able to take an 11-ton (10-tonne) load of cargo to the ISS.

An Orbiter's approach to the ISS is extremely slow and careful. Small steering rockets in the nose and tail make adjustments to the Orbiter's angle and position. Finally, the space plane links to the ISS using a special **docking** unit in the front of the cargo bay.

Construction of the ISS stopped in 2003, when the Space Shuttle *Columbia* broke up on its way back to Earth. Flights began again in 2005. Completing the ISS is the aim of the flights.

ORBITFACT
The Shuttle Orbiter's design makes it ideal for lifting big sections of the ISS. The cargo bay is 60 feet (18.3 meter) long and 15 feet (4.6 meter) wide, so an ISS module fits inside. The Orbiter can take up to 25 tons (22.7 tonnes) into orbit.

Glides like a brick

The Shuttle Orbiter may have wings, but they do not give it any great soaring abilities. The landing approach is flown precisely along a computer-controlled flight path, to allow the Orbiter to land on a runway. Once the Orbiter leaves orbit, the space plane glides to the ground without any rocket or jet engines.

Rocket
escape
system

Protective
shroud

Russian space taxi

The reliable Soyuz rocket carries new crews and supplies to the ISS.

Russia's Soyuz, or "Union," spacecraft is smaller than the Space Shuttle, and is a much older design, dating back to the 1960s. Soyuz has three sections: an orbital module, a **re-entry** module, and a service module. The service module has solar panels and radio systems, as well as rockets for propulsion and steering. The Soyuz carries up to three cosmonauts, with an air supply for just over three days. The orbital module contains the docking port, necessary for linking to the Space Station.

◄ The Soyuz spacecraft is protected during launch by a large shroud, or covering. In an emergency, a rocket escape system lifts cosmonauts to safety.

▼ A Soyuz spacecraft has three modules, with power being supplied by solar panel "wings."

Orbital module with
docking probe at front

Re-entry module and
crew compartment

Equipment module and
power supply

ORBITFACT
Mir showed that emergencies can happen. ISS always has a Soyuz space "lifeboat" docked, in case the crew has to leave the station fast. In **stand-by mode**, fuel and power on a Soyuz last about 200 days. After that, a new one is flown up.

▲ Soyuz uses a spear-like probe to dock with the ISS.

◀ A Soyuz docked to the ISS. Behind it, another spacecraft is also docked. This is a Progress cargo ship.

◀ Astronaut Jeffrey Williams shows the snug fit of the Soyuz cabin. There is room for two more crew to sit next to him.

Mission Control

ISS operations are run by ground controllers in the U.S. and in Russia. The experts in a control room range from the Flight Surgeon, who checks on the crew's health, to the EVA Systems Officer, who is in charge of **space walks** and the ISS **robot** arm.

Mission control room at the Houston Space Flight Center in the U.S.

Satellites beam signals between the ISS and mission controllers

Approaches to the ISS can be carried out either under computer control, or with the pilot in command. It is a nose-first flight maneuver, with the docking probe of the orbital module aimed at a matching port on the ISS.

When the docking is complete, the center of the probe is removed. Cosmonauts and equipment can then pass freely into the ISS.

Robot rockets

Automatic spacecraft also make supply flights to the ISS, keeping it stocked with vital provisions needed by the crew.

▲ An astronaut's-eye view of a Progress cargo ship making its final approach to the ISS. Progress was developed from the crewed Soyuz, and looks similar.

The Progress spacecraft is Russia's standard cargo carrier. It is uncrewed, and docks with the ISS under computer control. Once firmly attached, the docking probe is removed, and ISS crew members can climb through the circular hole to unload the cargo. Three to four Progress flights are made each year.

▼ Various items packed into Progress 18's hatch after docking with the ISS.

The Automated Transfer Vehicle (ATV) is Europe's automated cargo ship. It is bigger than Progress, and can carry ten tons (nine tonnes) of supplies, which is about three times more. Like Progress, it can fire small thruster rockets when docked to the ISS, allowing it to push the station gently up to a slightly higher orbit.

A shroud protects the ATV during launch from Earth

▲ The ATV makes a completely automatic approach to the ISS.

Fully loaded, the ATV weighs 23 tons (20.7 tonnes) at launch

▲ The Progress
cargo spacecraft
(left) compared
with the bigger
ATV (right). They
both have the
same docking
probe design.

◀ Cosmonaut
Sergei Krikalev
holds a Progress
docking probe
after it has safely
attached to the
ISS. Now crew
can unload
the supplies.

ORBITFACT
Progress is another
Russian old-timer of space.
Every space station except
Skylab has been supplied by
Progress cargo craft. Like the
Soyuz, Progress has been
updated over the years, and
more than 110 of them
have flown.

Where does the garbage go?

Even with a crew of only three aboard, plenty
of trash is created after a stay on the ISS. The
ISS is not a roomy environment, and whether
the garbage is old technical equipment, food
scraps, or toilet waste, it all has to go
somewhere. So far, the main "trash can" has
been the Progress spacecraft. Once supplies
have been unloaded, waste is put aboard the re-
entry module. This breaks up as it hits the upper
atmosphere, and disposes of the unwanted cargo.
The ATV will do the same on its return flights,
getting rid of up to six tons (5.5 tonnes) of waste.

The scorching heat of re-entry breaks up
"trash can" spacecraft. Any surviving
pieces fall into the Pacific Ocean

Space builders

The modules of the ISS are built on Earth, but astronauts are needed for final assembly in orbit.

When it is finished, construction of the ISS will have taken about 1200 hours of Extra-Vehicular Activity (EVA), or space walks. Each EVA lasts several hours. Astronauts wear space suits that are equipped with life support, such as heating, cooling, air supply, and radio equipment.

▲ The Quest airlock was installed in 2001. It was needed because U.S. and Russian hatches had different designs and would not work together. It can hold two suited-up astronauts at a time.

▶ Astronauts float into the Quest module before starting a space walk.

Astronauts cannot just open a hatch and leave the ISS, otherwise the air from inside would rush out into space. Instead a double-door **airlock** is used. The main airlock on the ISS is the Quest module. It has an inner and outer hatch. When the inner hatch is shut, an outer hatch can be opened, which allows astronauts to float into space.

◀ Space helmets have a gold-tinted faceplate (1) to cut down the Sun's glare. Helmet lights are used when the ISS passes into the Earth's shadow. Astronauts are tethered (2) to stop them from floating away. Here, a foot restraint (3) is used. U.S. suits (4) are made in top and bottom halves, joined at the waist. The backpack (5) provides life support for up to eight hours.

ORBITFACT
Two kinds of space suits are used on the ISS. The U.S. Extra-vehicular Mobility Unit (EMU) comes in upper and lower halves, joined at the waist. The Russian Orlan, or Sea Eagle, suit is a one-piece design, with an entry hatch in the back.

▲ Astronauts working on the main truss in 2006, while tethered safely to the ISS structure.

▼ An EMU suit has a safety system in case a tether cable snaps. The Simplified Aid for Extravehicular activity Rescue (SAFER) fits around the backpack and has small gas-jets to push it slowly around in space. Using a chest-mounted control, an astronaut could return safely to the ISS.

Chest control

SAFER unit

What use is an old space suit?

Suitsat came from an idea to reuse a worn-out Orlan space suit for educational purposes. The helmet of the space suit was fitted with a radio beacon. On Earth, a Russian science team recorded messages from students across the world. The empty space suit began playing the recordings when it was launched from the ISS in February 2006. Students could tune in on radios to hear the faint recordings for about two weeks as Suitsat orbited Earth.

Suitsat before launch, with radio beacon on helmet

Space scientists

▲ Science on the ISS covers research in many areas. These include making special drugs (1) and growing plants (2, 3). Tracking the Earth (4) is important – here a volcano is shown – as are experiments in human biology (5, 6).

Carrying out experiments is one of the key reasons for building the ISS. The Destiny module was built as the U.S. space laboratory.

Destiny is the first U.S. orbital research center since Skylab of 1973-1974. Destiny was launched into space aboard the Shuttle Orbiter *Atlantis* in 2001. Scientists will be able to work in the module for about ten years, when constant wear and tear will make it due for repair or replacement.

Destiny is an **aluminum** tube 28 feet (8.5 meter) long, containing 24 equipment racks. These are for experiments, and for power, cooling, and life-support systems. A European-made freezer unit allows various lab samples to be stored at four different temperatures. These range from just above freezing to -112°F (-80°C), which is essential for some experiments.

Floating in space

The weightless environment of the ISS makes many jobs easy to carry out. For example, spindly robot arms can move loads that would be impossibly heavy on Earth.

Science experiments are aimed at finding out whether some things can be done better in space than on Earth.

The Destiny module being moved by a robot arm

Astronaut Marsha Ivins shows the effect of weightlessness on her long hair

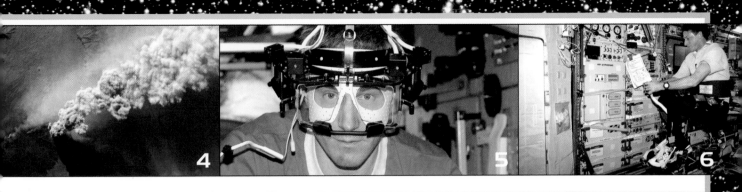

Studying the Earth's environment is an important part of Destiny's role. Destiny has a special porthole, named the Window Observational Research Facility (WORF), made from four layers of glass. A metal shutter swings across, to protect the WORF when no one is using it.

△ One end of the Destiny laboratory links to the Unity connecting module. Unity was the first U.S.-made part of the ISS to go into orbit, in 1998.

ORBITFACT
Life-support systems on the ISS are essential for the crew's survival, and clean air is a part of that. Electric fans suck away fumes and gases given off by experiments. Filters remove the waste gas exhaled by the crew.

◀ Astronaut Jeffrey Williams takes pictures through the Destiny window. Williams was the ISS science officer and flight engineer in 2006.

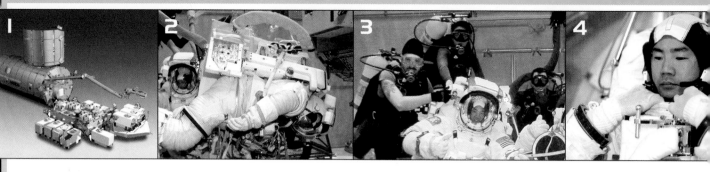

▲ Japan's Experimental Module (JEM) is named Kibo, or "Hope" (1). A Japanese astronaut trains in an underwater tank (2). Floating underwater simulates the weightless environment of space. Divers stand by (3) in case a space suit springs a leak. In 2005 Soichi Noguchi (4) became the first Japanese astronaut.

International effort

Hundreds of companies make the parts to build the ISS. The parts range from entire modules to smaller items, such as windows and laboratory equipment.

The five space agencies in charge of the ISS come from all over the world. The ISS's construction has been a big test for an international partnership. Money has been a big issue, for the ISS will cost $100 billion by the time it is finished. For the companies involved, the technical advances make the project worthwhile.

Cupola is made mostly of aluminum and glass. On Earth it weighs almost two tons (1.8 tonnes)

The Cupola has a computer workstation, lights, and window heaters

◀ The Cupola dome was made in Italy. It has six windows and a porthole. The Cupola is useful for checking nearby spacecraft and for controlling the ISS robot arm. It can also be used to look at the Earth and other space objects.

Covers shut to protect the windows when the Cupola is not being used

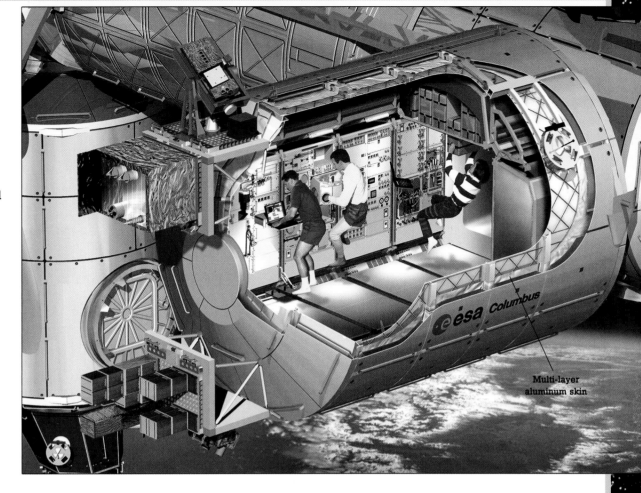

► Columbus has rows of standard-sized racks, packed with research equipment.

Multi-layer aluminum skin

The Columbus module is another ISS laboratory. It was built by a group of European companies, headed by a German company. Like other ISS modules, Columbus was designed to fit inside a Space Shuttle cargo bay, and has a multi-layer aluminum skin. This acts as lightweight armor, for protection from collisions with stray objects speeding through space.

It is very busy out in space!

Space stations are not alone in orbit. Since Sputnik 1 was launched in 1957, thousands of objects have been sent into space. Many of them now form a junkyard in the sky. Such space junk includes old fuel tanks, discarded parts, and even flecks of paint.

The screen (left) shows a picture of the larger pieces in space. More than 500,000 items bigger than your finger are believed to be in orbit, though no one knows the exact figure. Any of them could be deadly if they hit a spacecraft.

Each dot shows a piece of orbiting space junk

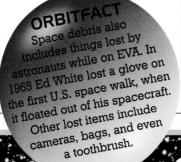

ORBITFACT
Space debris also includes things lost by astronauts while on EVA. In 1965 Ed White lost a glove on the first U.S. space walk, when it floated out of his spacecraft. Other lost items include cameras, bags, and even a toothbrush.

Amazing arms

Long robot arms are among the most useful tools for carrying out jobs on the ISS.

The Space Station's main robot arm is the Mobile Servicing System (MSS), or Canadarm2, which was transported from Earth by the Space Shuttle *Endeavour* in 2001. The robot arm was built in Canada. Attached to the ISS, the arm's movements are controlled by ISS crew from workstations in the Destiny laboratory module. Unlike a human arm, Canadarm2 has several "elbows," giving it tremendous flexibility. The arm's mobile base system allows it to move around the ISS.

Mobile base system

Canadarm2 is far longer than any human arm, extending to 57.7 feet (17.6 meter), with seven motorized joints. Using the arm, controllers can move equipment and supplies around the ISS, as well as service various instruments fixed to the outside.

▲ Leroy Chiao controls Canadarm2 using a three-screen video workstation in the Destiny module.

◀ Stephen Robinson uses the Canadarm2 to make repairs to the Space Shuttle's heat protection tiles. The 2005 flight was the first Shuttle mission since the loss of the *Columbia* during re-entry, two years before.

Foot restraint

On Earth the arm weighs just over 1.8 tons (1.6 tonnes)

The station's arm is strong enough to be used as a mobile platform for astronauts working in space. Video cameras and lights give the arm's operator in the Destiny module a clear view as work progresses.

Avoiding another disaster

In 2003 the Space Shuttle *Columbia* was destroyed as it re-entered the Earth's atmosphere, and all seven crew members were killed. The accident was caused by damage to the Orbiter's left wing during takeoff, though no one had noticed this at the time. During re-entry, super-hot air blasted into the wing and the craft blew apart.

All Shuttle flights were stopped, while experts figured out ways to improve safety. One of the improvements was to make the Orbiter's own robot arm longer, with a video camera at the end. Using this, Shuttle crews can inspect the delicate heat protection system in space, to check that it is in good condition for a safe re-entry. If not, repairs can be made by an astronaut on EVA.

Heat protection tiles cover the bottom of the Shuttle

Video camera on the end of the arm

Life aboard the ISS

▲ Flight engineer Susan Helms (left) and mission commander Yury Usachev float in the Destiny module (1). Moving hefty bags is easy in space (2). After work, each crew member has their own personal sleep station (3).

▼ Exercise is a daily chore (4) but is essential to keep muscles in good condition. Drinks are stored in sealed pouches (5) to stop stray liquid floating into equipment and causing a fault.

Each ISS crew spends about six months on board the Station. Space tourists have also joined them for shorter periods.

Space Station crews work every day according to schedules made up with mission control on Earth. Days are never exactly alike, but they normally start at about 6.00 a.m. with an inspection, using laptop computers, to check that all ISS systems are working properly. Washing up takes half an hour, and is followed by a 50-minute break for breakfast. After this, there is a fifteen-minute planning session with ground control.

▲ The first female tourist to the ISS was Anousheh Ansari, who spent eight days in the station in 2006.

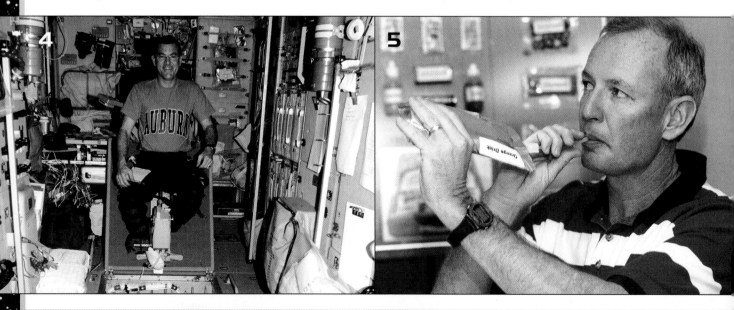

3

Astronaut John Phillips works on an Elektron oxygen generator

Oxygen from water

The air on the ISS is as near to that of the Earth as possible. It is a mixture of the two main gases we breathe, **oxygen** and nitrogen.

The oxygen is made by Russian Elektron generators, which split water fed into them into its two parts, oxygen and hydrogen. The oxygen is used for breathing, while the hydrogen is a waste product, and is released into space.

The water used by an Elektron is mostly waste, either from washing or from the crew's own urine. Elektrons are not always reliable. When there is a failure, bottled oxygen is used. There is also a supply of cylinders that make oxygen from stored chemicals.

Preparation for the day's work takes about half an hour. Jobs may include science experiments or studying the Earth. Space walks are much more elaborate and have separate planning sessions.

Physical exercise is vital to stay in shape, and all crew members have to complete at least two-and-a-half hours a day working out on the various exercise machines. Checking life-support equipment is also a daily necessity. Forty minutes is allowed for the inspection. Towards the end of the day, work reports have to be filed, followed by another planning meeting with ground control. Bedtime is officially at 9:30 p.m., but crews often stay up later to chat, watch a movie, or swap e-mails with family and friends.

▼ ISS mealtimes (6) give an important social break as well as food.

Visitors leave mission badges to mark their time on the ISS (7).

6

7

ORBITFACT
The first astronauts ate paste out of squeeze tubes, and pre-packaged bite-sized chunks of food. Today, tasty items are much in demand. For example, a Swedish astronaut visiting the ISS took dried moose meat, crispbread, and ginger cookies to eat.

New frontiers

New spacecraft are being developed to make flights to orbit easier and cheaper. There are even plans to build an orbiting hotel for space vacations.

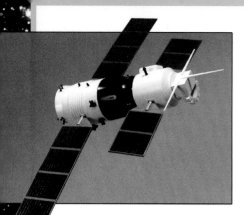

▲ The Chinese Shenzhou spacecraft is based on Russia's Soyuz, but is bigger all around. It uses the same three-module layout as Soyuz, but has two sets of solar panels.

▼ Orion will be launched by a rocket based on the Space Shuttle's solid rocket booster. The long, thin rocket has been nicknamed "the stick."

More countries plan to be in the space business in the future. Chief among the newcomers is China, with its Shenzhou spacecraft. China's first astronaut went into space in 2003, and future plans include a permanent space station, based on Shenzhou modules left in orbit.

The U.S. Space Shuttles will go out of service by 2010. Their replacement is the Orion, a "capsule" style of crewed spacecraft, similar to the Apollo that was designed in the 1960s.

Cone-shaped crew capsule, with room for up to six astronauts

Rocket escape system in case of launch emergency

Orion is a much smaller and simpler design than the Shuttle Orbiter, and has room for just six astronauts. Heavy cargo loads will not be carried in the Orion. They will be launched into space by a separate, uncrewed rocket.

▶ A possible future view from an ISS porthole, as a Kliper approaches.

Russian space plans include the six-seater Kliper, a space plane that looks much like a smaller version of the Shuttle Orbiter. The Kliper will be made of several modules, including a winged re-entry craft, a "people pod," and a service module at the back.

Final approach to the ISS will be backwards, because Kliper's docking probe is behind the crew module. Russia may also use the craft on future missions to the Moon and perhaps even further one day, on a flight to Mars.

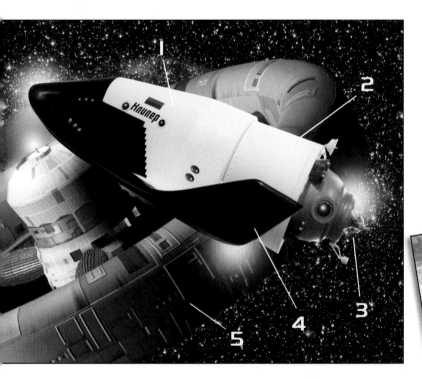

▲ Kliper has a six-seat crew pod (1), and a docking module (2). The docking probe (3) is at the back. The wings have fins at the tips (4). This space station is a space wheel (5) design.

Blow-up space hotel

Several space tourists have already visited the ISS. Space technology company Bigelow Aerospace has plans for a future space hotel. The Bigelow Genesis 1 module went into orbit in 2006 to test the idea of an inflatable space structure, much like a high-tech, but far stronger, balloon. The module performed very well. Bigelow believes that future versions of the Genesis could be the start of vacations in space.

Picture taken by a camera mounted on the outside of Genesis 1

Genesis 1 is 14.4 feet (4.4 meter) long

Timeline

Here are discoveries and achievements marking missions in orbit – from first ideas to giant space stations of the future.

▲ Salyut 7 was launched in 1982.

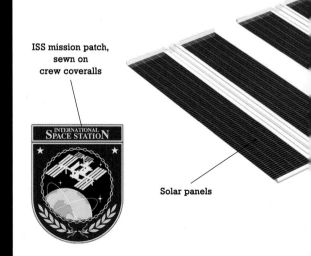

▲ Tsiolkovsky was a math teacher who wrote many books on space travel. He sketched designs for rockets and space stations. He even thought of growing plants aboard spacecraft, to provide food, and oxygen to breathe.

1857 Konstantin Tsiolkovsky is born in Russia. He is the first person to work out many of the basics of space flight, including orbital speeds and the idea of space stations. In 1911 he writes a letter in which he says, "*Earth is the cradle of humanity but one cannot live in the cradle forever.*"

1869 U.S. author Edward Everett Hale writes *The Brick Moon*, the first book to feature a space station. In the story, the "Moon" is a sphere 200 feet (60 meter) across. During the launch, its builders and their families are accidentally carried away from the Earth – but they adapt well to their new life in space.

1957 The first spacecraft, called Sputnik 1, is launched. It weighs 184 pounds (83.6 kilograms), and orbits the Earth once every 96 minutes.

1961 On April 12, Yuri Gagarin becomes the first human in space, making one orbit of the Earth, in the spacecraft Vostok 1.

1967 The first crewed flight of the Soyuz spacecraft. Improved and updated versions of the same design are still used to fly to and from the International Space Station.

1968 The movie *2001: A Space Odyssey* is released. Director Stanley Kubrick shows a huge wheel-shaped space station, plus various other items of realistic-looking space hardware.

1971 Salyut 1 is launched to become the first space station. It is about 45 feet (13.7 meters) long, and weighs 44 tons (40 tonnes). More Salyut stations are built after this. The last one, called Salyut 7, is launched in 1982.

1973 Skylab becomes the first U.S. station. The 84-ton (76-tonne) craft stays in orbit from 1973 to 1979. Three crews stay in 1973 and 1974.

1978 The Progress cargo spacecraft makes its first flight, on a Soyuz rocket. Progress was developed from the crewed Soyuz spacecraft, and helps resupply the ISS today.

1981 The first orbital flight of the U.S. Space Shuttle occurs when the *Columbia* lifts off from the Kennedy Space Center in Florida. It makes 37 orbits of the Earth, during which it covers a distance of about 1,074,567 miles (1.7 million kilometers).

1986 The first section of the Mir space station is sent into orbit. Various modules are added from 1986 to 1996, during which time Mir is lived in and visited by astronauts from many countries.

1993 The ISS project is announced, at first called Space Station Alpha. It combines ideas from several proposed but unbuilt stations, such as the U.S. Space Station Freedom, Russia's Mir-2, and the European Columbus space laboratory.

1998 The first ISS sections, the Russian Zarya and the U.S. Unity modules, are assembled in orbit.

2000 In July, the Russian Zvezda module is added to Zarya and Unity, and people go aboard the ISS. It has a minimum crew of two, and from now on the ISS is occupied continuously.

The completed ISS

This is the layout of the finished International Space Station, when it will have a full crew of six people. The ISS is an expensive project, but it is also a fine example of how scientists, technicians, companies, and nations can work together towards a common goal.

ISS mission patch, sewn on crew coveralls

Solar panels

2001 Braking rockets are fired to slow down the Mir space station, bringing it down from orbit.

2001 The Destiny laboratory is added to the ISS, as is the Quest airlock module, and the Pirs docking module below Zvezda. Other assembly work includes adding sections of the main truss.

2001 Canadarm2 is installed aboard the ISS.

2003 Space Shuttle *Columbia* breaks up during re-entry, and all the crew are killed. The loss puts a two-year stop to ISS construction, while Shuttle designers improve its safety.

2003 The first Chinese astronaut, or taikonaut, flies into space aboard the Shenzhou rocket.

2005 Shuttle assembly flights start again.

2006 Anousheh Ansari becomes the first female space tourist. Three other tourists have flown before Ansari – Dennis Tito (2001), Mark Shuttleworth (2002) and Gregory Olsen (2005).

2006 The Bigelow Genesis 1 inflatable module is sent into space. The aim is to test the idea, before launching a bigger "space hotel" version.

2007 The European ATV makes its first flight, and the Columbus laboratory is attached to the ISS.

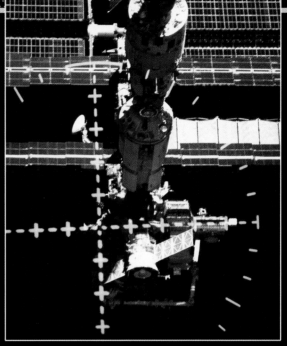

◄ A view from the Shuttle *Discovery*, as it leaves the ISS in August 2001. The green markings are part of the aiming system that allows Shuttle pilots to dock with the ISS.

2009 The Japanese Kibo, and a Russian laboratory module are attached to the ISS.

2010 and beyond Plans for the ISS to be complete. Space Shuttles make their last flights, and are replaced by the smaller Orion capsule. Russia's Kliper space plane flies, and China develops a space station.

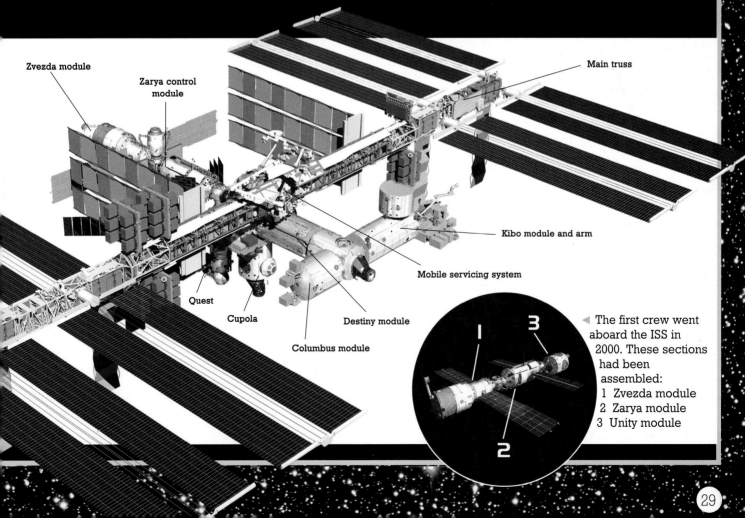

Zvezda module

Zarya control module

Main truss

Kibo module and arm

Mobile servicing system

Quest

Cupola

Destiny module

Columbus module

◄ The first crew went aboard the ISS in 2000. These sections had been assembled:
1 Zvezda module
2 Zarya module
3 Unity module

Glossary

Here are explanations of many of the technical terms used in this book.

◄ The Space Shuttle has two solid-fuel boosters, used at takeoff.

Airlock A two-door system that lets an astronaut enter or leave a spacecraft, without losing air into space. The inner door is sealed shut before the outer door is opened. This ensures that little or no air escapes into space.

Aluminum A silvery-gray metal that is light but strong, and resists rust. It is widely used for building aircraft, and for the modules of the ISS.

▲ The outer hatch of the Quest airlock is opened at the start of an ISS space walk.

Antenna A rod- or dish-shaped aerial that transmits or receives radio and TV signals.

Artificial satellite A spacecraft orbiting the Earth or other space object, such as the Moon. At least 4000 artificial satellites have been launched into space since Sputnik 1 of 1957.

Atmosphere The layers of gases that surround many planets. Earth's air is a mixture of mostly nitrogen and oxygen.

Cosmonaut Russian name for a space traveler. Most countries use the U.S. term astronaut.

Docking Describes two spacecraft linking together. Crewed craft have a hatchway so that astronauts can move from one spacecraft to another.

Equator An imaginary circle around the Earth, halfway between the North and South poles.

Flare A violent explosion of gas and radiation from the surface of the Sun.

Inclined orbit An orbit between the equator and the poles.

Life support The machinery that allows a human to function in space. Life support equipment supplies air, heating and cooling, food and water, physical protection, and deals with bodily waste.

Main truss In the ISS, the main truss is the backbone structure that carries the various modules and the solar panels.

Module A section of a spacecraft. Examples are crew, cargo, or communications modules.

Orbit The curving path one space object takes around a larger one. The Earth orbits the Sun once a year, and the Moon orbits the Earth every 27.3 days. The ISS orbits the Earth every 90-93 minutes. The exact time it takes per orbit varies a little because of small changes in orbital height.

Oxygen The life-giving gas in the air we breathe in. When we exhale, we breathe out carbon dioxide gas, as waste. On the ISS, oxygen is made by Elektron machines, which split waste water into its two parts, oxygen and hydrogen.

Radiation The range of wave energy found in nature. Visible light is one example, as are invisible infra-red heat rays. High-energy radiation from the Sun damages living cells.

Radiator Any device that gives off heat. Unlike the radiators in a house, which give off heat into a room to warm it up, radiators on a spacecraft radiate heat away from it out into space to help keep it cool.

Re-entry Coming back into the Earth's atmosphere after a space mission.

Robot A machine that can carry out a series of complex orders without a human operator. Strictly speaking, the robot arms of the ISS are not robots at all, since they are controlled by humans.

Solar panel A panel covered with silicon that converts the energy in light into electricity.

Solid-rocket booster (SRB) A rocket that burns a solid mixture rather than a liquid fuel. Generally, boosters are one or more extra rockets that increase the lifting power of the main rocket at takeoff. Boosters drop away when their fuel is used up, usually a minute or two after takeoff.

Soyuz Russia's crewed spacecraft, which has been in service since the 1970s.

Space agency A government organization in charge of space research. The U.S. space agency is National Aeronautics and Space Administration (NASA).

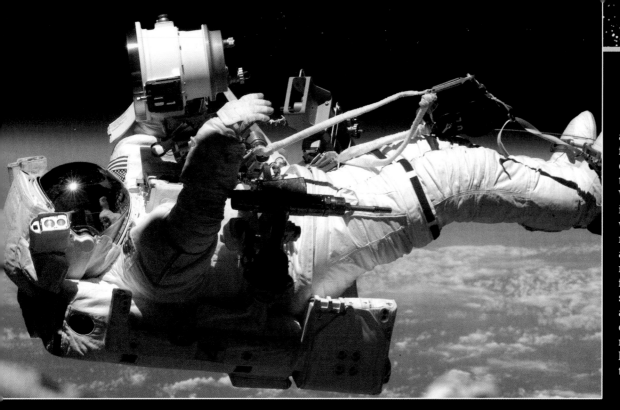

Space plane A spacecraft with wings, rather than having a capsule shape.

Space Shuttle NASA's crewed spacecraft, used since the early 1980s. Consists of a winged Orbiter space plane, a large fuel tank, and two rocket boosters used for takeoff. The Shuttle carries the main modules of the ISS into orbit.

Space tourist Someone who can pay for a private space flight. A ticket costs more than $20 million for a ten-day trip to the ISS.

Space walk Floating in space outside a spacecraft, while wearing a space suit. Also called Extra-Vehicular Activity, or EVA.

Sputnik Word used for early spacecraft, meaning "fellow traveller," or satellite.

Stand-by mode A stand-by mode shuts down a machine's main systems, but keeps them ready for action, if needed. Stand-by mode does take up some energy, and eventually fresh fuel is needed.

Thrust The force that pushes an aircraft forward.

Vacuum Empty of matter, so that there is no air.

Weightless Floating in space where there is no strong gravity field, or the force of attraction between objects.

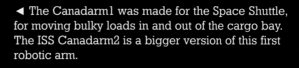

▲ Solar flares are vast eruptions of the Sun's surface. Here the Earth (arrowed) is shown to the same scale, next to the Sun.

◄ The Canadarm1 was made for the Space Shuttle, for moving bulky loads in and out of the cargo bay. The ISS Canadarm2 is a bigger version of this first robotic arm.

Index

Acknowledgements
We wish to thank all those people who have helped to create this publication. Information and images were supplied by:
Individuals:
    Jack Higgens
    Mat Irvine/Smallspace Photos
    David Jefferis
    Gavin Page/Design Shop
iStockphoto:
    Stephen Sweet
    Brian Shephard
Organizations:
    Alpha Archive
    Canadian Space Agency
    EADS
    ESA European Space Agency
    JAXA Japan Aerospace Exploration Agency
    NASA National Aeronautics and Space Administration
    Novosti Agency
    Science Museum London
    US Air Force

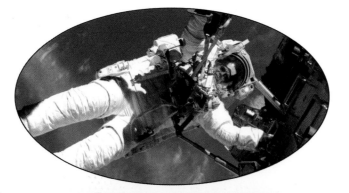

Printed in the U.S.A.